Hustling and Bustling
TRUCKS

FOX EYE
PUBLISHING

WHEELS AND AUTOMOBILES

A truck is a machine that does big, heavy jobs.

Trucks carry goods such as food, cars and logs.

flatbed trailer

Trucks are tough. Trucks are strong. Straight trucks are box shaped. Tractor-trailers are long.

Flatbed trailers have open sides. Which trucks are in this picture? How many can you find?

CB radio

The cab is where the driver sits when driving on the road.

Truck drivers talk to each other on CB radios.

Some trucks have a sleeping box
behind the driver's seat.

It has a bed and kitchen where
the driver sleeps and eats.

auto hauler

The street sweeper sweeps the street.
The dustbin lorry keeps it neat.

Auto haulers carry cars.
Trucks carry goods near and far.

power line

A cherry picker lifts some workers up into the sky.

It helps the workers reach and fix a broken power line.

Reefers are refrigerated trailers.
They carry frozen food.

reefer

As the food goes to the shops,
the reefer keeps it cool.

Concrete mixers mix concrete
as they travel along the road.

concrete mixer

Flatbed trailers are super strong.
They carry the heaviest loads.

layby ——

It's been a busy day, with so
many tasks along the way.

But now the jobs are done and the day is over.
It's time to park up in a layby stopover.

Tomorrow will soon be here,
with many more jobs to complete.

So in the driver's bed, behind the seat,
the driver lies down and goes to sleep!

Bustling Words

Concrete is a very tough, hard material used to build with.

Frozen describes something that is so cold it has become very hard.

Goods are things that people want or like.

A **layby** is an area at the side of a road in which vehicles can stop.

A **load** is something that is carried.

Logs are pieces of wood cut from trees.

A **machine** is something that helps us to do work.

Park means to put a vehicle somewhere.

A **reefer** is a truck with a refrigerator.

Refrigerated means kept cold.

Stopover means to stop for the night, or is a place in which you stop for the night.

Sweep means to clear away.

Tasks are jobs.

Travel means to move from one place to another.

First published in 2024 by Fox Eye Publishing
Unit 31, Vulcan House Business Centre,
Vulcan Road, Leicester, LE5 3EF
www.foxeyepublishing.com

Author: Katherine Eason
Art director: Paul Phillips
Cover designer: Emma Bailey
Editor: Jenny Rush

All illustrations by Eszter Szepvolgyi

978-1-80445-346-9

Printed in China